M000236261

be yourself dazzling
joyful imaginative juicy
bold strong zingy
vivacious quixotic
good creative daring
colorful happy well-
loved adventurous
dynamic true kooky

WORD PLAY QUILTS

Easy Techniques from the UnRuly Quilter

TONYA RICUCCI

Martingale®
& COMPANY

Word Play Quilts: Easy Techniques from
the UnRuly Quilter
© 2010 by Tonya Ricucci

That Patchwork Place® is an imprint of
Martingale & Company®.

Martingale & Company
19021 120th Ave. NE, Ste. 102
Bothell, WA 98011 USA
www.martingale-pub.com

Credits

President & CEO: Tom Wierzbicki
Editor in Chief: Mary V. Green
Managing Editor: Tina Cook
Design Director: Stan Green
Acquisitions & Developmental Editor:
    Karen Costello Soltys
Technical Editor: Darra Williamson
Copy Editor: Melissa Bryan
Production Manager: Regina Girard
Illustrator: Laurel Strand
Cover & Text Designer: Stan Green
Photographer: Brent Kane

Printed in China
15 14 13 12 11 10   8 7 6 5 4 3 2 1

**Library of Congress Cataloging-in-Publication Data
is available upon request.**

ISBN: 978-1-60468-017-1

Mission Statement
Dedicated to providing quality products and service
to inspire creativity.

CONTENTS

LIBERATED QUILTMAKING

"Liberated quiltmaking" is a phrase I began using two decades ago to describe a way of working that relied upon a process rather than a pattern. Instead of using conventional methods, I began exploring new ways of constructing blocks. Soon I found ways to make Log Cabin, Star, House, Shoo Fly, and other traditional blocks using these new nontraditional methods that eliminated patterns and templates.

In the beginning, I called this new method of quiltmaking "improvisational," "intuitive," "free-piecing," or "free-pieced," but finally settled on the adjective "liberated" because that was the way it always made me feel. It involved beginning a quilt with just a seed of an idea and letting the creation develop in a spontaneous way. Soon I was figuring out how to teach these new methods, which—I'm pleased to say—were received enthusiastically. The thing I've heard most frequently is that these methods give quilters the freedom to make their own quilts, and that's exactly right. It's all about freedom and self-expression. I've always thought of it as "playtime at the sewing machine."

Liberated quiltmaking is never boring, because you are not repeating the exact same thing over and over. Rather, you stay completely engaged throughout the entire project, making the next decision, and *then* the next, and *then* the next. Because you are thinking about it all the way through the process, I believe you make better decisions. As you work, you can change your mind about anything you like because you aren't following a pattern. The more you get done, the clearer the next decisions become. Almost everything is fixable if something goes wrong. When the quilt is finished, there is a great sense of accomplishment because *you* made all the decisions, and the result is, indeed, *your* quilt. That is a very fine experience.

Over the years, I've found that when I explain a Liberated process to my students, they quickly adjust it to their own way of working, which in turn results in work that is distinctly their own.

I have frequently used words in my quilt designs. Letters add yet another graphic element to quilts, and words are a splendid way to add a personal

"GWENNY'S FLOWER POT," 45" x 50", 2010, designed and made by Gwen Marston. Machine quilted by Robyn House.

touch. I have signed and dated many quilts with letters and numbers, and have memorialized many of my family's beloved pets by incorporating their names, but always with appliqué.

Since I first began playing with Liberated quiltmaking, I've continued to develop new ideas and refine old ones, but never once did I think of the possibility of free-pieced letters. I don't think anyone else had either. Tonya took the concept of Liberated quiltmaking and invented an entirely new process. Thanks to Tonya, I've added another process to my Liberated bag of tricks. The first time I experimented with Tonya's method for making free-pieced letters, I found myself completely engrossed in figuring out how to make them. Piecing letters is just a great idea. These pieced letters have a playful spirit that complements the kind of quilts I like to make.

Making letters using Tonya's Liberated methods is a great adventure into the magical world of Liberated quiltmaking. Now she has given us a delightful book with clear, easy-to-understand instructions. Nice work, Tonya!

~ *Gwen Marston*

INTRODUCTION

I love words on quilts, but none of the methods previously available
for creating them appealed to me.

Although I don't hate it, appliqué is not my passion. I do needle-turn appliqué, but it's slow and takes effort, and I'm too lazy to do that often. I hate fusible appliqué with a passion. I primarily hand quilt and that fusible web is a needle breaker. Raw-edged appliqué? Too messy, especially for the smaller block size that I gravitate to.

So . . . how about pieced alphabets? These always required measuring and following exact instructions. I'm really not good at that, plus the results looked static to me, too precise.

Then, in September 2000, while sewing Liberated houses from Gwen Marston's book *Liberated Quiltmaking* (see "Resources" on page 64), it struck me that I could use the same methods to make letters. Wheeeee!

After making a few free-pieced letters for that House quilt, I made "Alphabet Sampler" (page 49) using my newfound technique. I never would have come up with this technique without Gwen. Gwen taught me the joy of mismatched seams, chopped-off points, and quilts made without planning ahead. Her book showed me how to make blocks without relying on patterns. I learned by doing and redoing, each time making the blocks a bit differently. That wouldn't have happened if I had simply followed directions to cut fabric in certain sizes and sew pieces together in an exact way. That freedom to play and experiment led me to create UnRuly letters, and ultimately to write this book.

My best advice to you is to approach making these "wonky" letters with an open mind, knowing that the technique is different from much of what is out there in existing quilt literature. You can start with baby steps or just jump right in.

Everyone learns differently. Some quilters can look at the letters and start sewing without reading the directions. If that sounds like you, go for it! Others need more detailed instruction, and that's what I've provided. Make the letters according to the guidelines I offer . . . and then make them again, this time differently. Break the rules. Don't be afraid to make mistakes—that's how you learn.

Sewing Liberated houses led me to UnRuly letters. Where will UnRuliness take you?

Finally: The most important thing to do while making letters? The quilt below sums it up!

**"HAVE FUN," 23" x 22", 2009, designed, made, and
hand quilted in freehand fans by the author.**

CHOOSING THE RIGHT FABRICS

In this section, you'll get a feel for what types of fabric work well for letters
and what kinds of fabric make them tricky to read.

I use 100%-cotton fabric because it's easy to work with and is available in such amazing colors and prints. Cotton holds a crease well and doesn't fray or stretch too much. Its medium weight also makes it ideal for hand quilting.

I have a friend who does lovely work mixing linens and silks along with woven and printed cottons. UnRuly piecing is forgiving, so don't restrict yourself to cotton if you like to work with other kinds of fabric; however, I'd avoid polyester and spandex because of their stretchiness.

I love working with two-sided fabric such as hand-dyes, solids, and batiks. You'll have one less thing to worry about when you can use either side of the fabric.

Contrast

I'm no expert when it comes to color, contrast, value, tints, and all that. It's easier just to show you with concrete examples what seems to work and what doesn't. Imagine that you are creating a flyer to advertise a quilt show—you want people to be able to read it.

> Black words on white have high contrast and are easy to read.

> Getting harder to read.

> Black letters on a dark background are hard to read. This is too low contrast.

> This is also low contrast because there isn't enough difference between the two colors.

Beware of Busy Prints

UnRuly letters in quilts aren't as straightforward as text on a page. Sewn letters have seams, the fabrics might be patterned, *and* unless you quilt around each letter, there will be quilting designs as well.

I've learned through trial and error that busy prints make for hard-to-read letters. Especially difficult are prints with equal amounts of contrasting colors. Diagonals and checks are problematic—on complicated letters all the unmatched patterns can make your eyes cross. Take a look at some of the examples on page 7 of what not to do!

"STAR LIGHT," 33½" x 42½", **2002, designed and made by the author. Tacked and hand quilted with embroidery floss. This is one of my early letter quilts, and it doesn't have nearly enough contrast. That's a lot of work only to end up without the impact I had hoped for.**

UnRuly letters made with busy prints are hard to read.

You don't necessarily want to use a busy fabric for the background either.

If you use fabric with a strong directional or one-way pattern, the print will run vertically as well as horizontally.

This cat fabric is a directional, or one-way, print, so it was difficult to use for letters. I managed not to put any cats standing on their heads, but there are quite a few lying sideways. To get all the cats facing upright, I could have cut strips crosswise (selvage to selvage) as well as lengthwise (along the selvage).

I much prefer to use novelty prints where they can really shine, such as the center of the letter O.

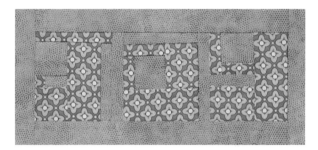

The fabric combination in this little block turned out to be a wonderful surprise. It's always worth experimenting. Sometimes an individual fabric or a fabric pairing works much better than expected.

Don't stress about getting the perfect fabric combinations. If you make what I call a "practice and repeat" quilt (making the same letters over and over again), you can try different fabrics and see what works for you. Each letter doesn't need to be legible; that's why it's such a good exercise.

The same goes for making a brick-style quilt (see "Introducing Word Bricks" on page 44). If a few bricks fall away, it doesn't matter because enough will be legible for the quilt message to hold up.

Fabric for Letters

Let's look at just a few options for letter fabric. Of course, there are many other possibilities.

Just Two Fabrics

Using just one fabric for all the letters and one *contrasting* fabric for all their backgrounds is the easiest option. The result is quite readable, as you can see in Rachael Thomas's quilt "Georgia, Georgia" (below).

Just Two Colors

Similar to the "just two fabrics" idea, this option uses the same fabric for all background pieces, but many fabrics—all of the same color—for the letters. This is the choice Julie Sefton made in "Flying Monkeys" (below).

"GEORGIA, GEORGIA," 36" x 42", 2009, designed, made, and hand quilted by Rachael Thomas. All letters are black on a medium-green background.

"FLYING MONKEYS," 61" x 86", 2008, designed and pieced by Julie Sefton. Machine quilted by Chris Ballard. Julie used a different yellow fabric for each word, but one consistent background fabric.

Same Fabric for Each Letter

In my quilt "Sensational" (below), I used a single black fabric for the letters and a multitude of tone-on-tone fabrics in various colors for the background. People often find this quilt difficult to read. Some letters have more than one background fabric and the backgrounds don't provide enough contrast with the black. I've since used this method more successfully by sticking to a single fabric for the background of each letter and for the adjacent spacer. I'll talk more about spacers later.

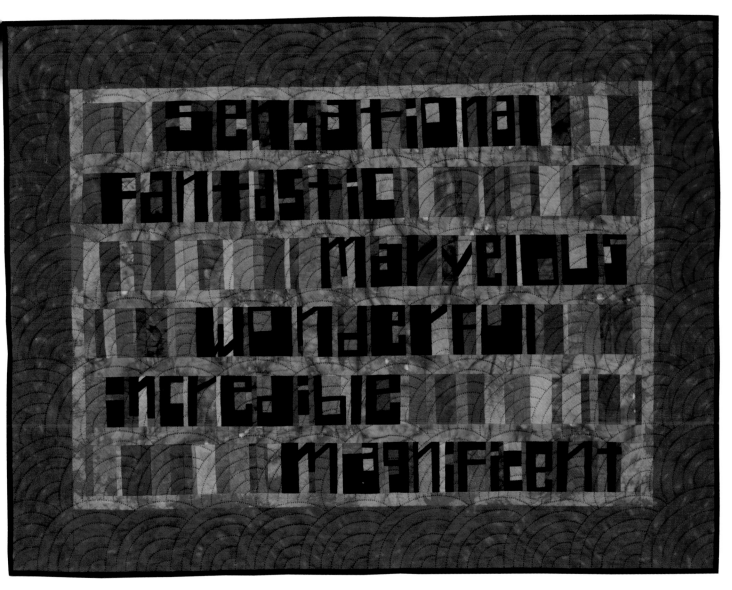

"SENSATIONAL," 48" x 26½", 2003, designed, made, and hand quilted in freehand fans with pearl cotton by the author.

Different Fabric for Each Letter

For "Alien Invasion" (below), I used a solid black for the background and assorted tone-on-tone brights for the letters. The letters in each word are made with such contrasting colors that I was able to snug them up against each other without using spacers.

Whenever possible, stagger the letters so that they "dance" up and down; the varying heights make them easier to see. I did a good job of that on "invasion" and "you" but could have done much better on "Alien" and "Planet"—those Ls definitely should have jogged up higher.

Scrappy Letters

Contrast becomes even more important if you make your letters scrappy. If one component of a letter is much stronger than the others, the letter may be hard to read or even look like a completely different letter—an F instead of an E, for instance. Using a very strong, consistent background fabric, such as the white I used in "Have Fun" (page 5), can help.

"ALIEN INVASION," 38½" x 45¼", 2003, designed and pieced by the author. Machine quilted by Bonnie K. Hunter. The stars were made using Gwen Marston's Liberated Variable Stars technique.

CUTTING STRIPS

The cut width of the fabric strips has a big impact on the look of your letters.
It's possible to free-piece letters using whatever scraps and strings you have
on hand, but it's *much easier* to start with strips precut just for this purpose.

I cut strips approximately ⅞" or 1", 1½", 2", and sometimes 2½" wide. I don't make them exact unless I need to for a specific project. Occasionally I'll need a strip wider than 2½"—to make an *X*, for example—but I wait until I need it to cut a strip that wide.

If I don't think I'll use much of a particular fabric, I cut only two strips (maybe a few extra if the strips aren't long). For a fabric I expect I'll use a lot, I cut one strip in each of the five widths listed, and I might even cut additional strips at varying widths. Just for fun, I sometimes angle my ruler so strips are wider at one end than at the other.

I'll admit: I am the queen of V-cut strips. This happens if you haven't folded the fabric straight when cutting a strip. No problem! Just slice the strip in two where the bend appears, and you'll be fine. If the ruler slips while you're cutting a strip (making the width vary), that's OK too.

Don't worry about V-cut strips when free-piecing letters.

If you're experimenting and don't want to commit to cutting lots of strips, cut a 10" square from the desired fabric and divide that into a bunch of short strips. Another option is to cut a 3½"-wide strip from the width of your fabric (approximately 40"), cut it into two, three, or four shorter lengths, and then cut those segments into narrower strips.

You don't always need multiple widths of letter and background fabric, but varying the widths will make a difference in how the letters look. I made "Joyful" (below) to show the dramatic impact strip width has on the finished letters. The cut strips varied in width between ⅞" and 2½".

"JOYFUL," 32¼" x 33½", 2010, designed, made, and hand quilted in freehand fans by the author. Thick or thin, straight or wonky, I made every one of these letters using the same method described in "Making Letters and Numbers" (page 19). Even a simple letter like *O* can be changed by using strips of various widths.

STRIP STORAGE? SIMPLE!
I hate how stringy and tangled strips get if they're not kept in line. I store my strips in baggies, putting all the strips of one fabric in a single sandwich-sized bag. I stick these baggies in bigger bags and containers, some sorted by color or theme.

It's not just the strip width that makes a difference in how the letters look, but also how you use the strips. In the detail below, which shows the top two middle blocks, I used just ⅞"-wide strips for the letters; however, the word on the bottom looks quite different because the letters are tall and skinny. Look at the center of the O: I used a square in the top and bottom block and a very long, narrow rectangle in the middle block.

USING THOSE LEFTOVERS

There are always great things to do with leftover strips.

- Piece them together to make a piano-key border like Julie Sefton did in "And Sometimes Y" also see page 52).
- Pass them along to a friend!
- Make a string quilt or block to donate to charity. The Heartstrings Quilt Project has great ideas for getting started. Visit their website at www.heartstringsquiltproject.com.

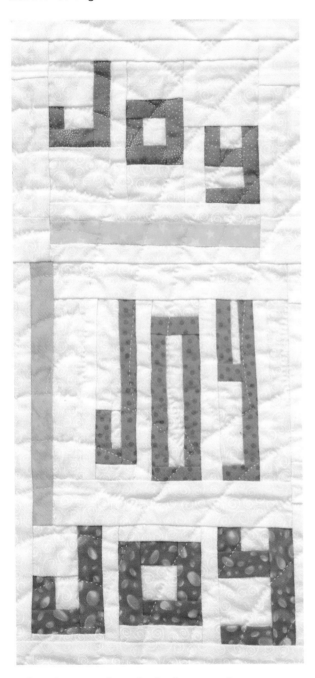

Believe it or not, the strips in the top and middle words are the same width, but the height and width of the letters creates a dramatic difference.

UNRULY LETTER BASICS

In this section you'll find basic information about terminology, tools, and supplies, as well as the methods that work best for me. Even if you've free-pieced before, I recommend at least skimming through the section; it probably contains a couple of techniques that may be new to you.

During the early phases of construction, there is no "proper size" for a strip, unit, or block. Nothing has to be just right. Enjoy the bobbles, the imperfections, and the lines that aren't straight. *You are making this quilt, not a robot!*

Terms to Know

You'll be seeing a few key terms a lot in the pages that follow. It will help to familiarize yourself with them now, or to mark this page for easy reference.

UnRuly piecing: sewing that involves as few *rules* and as little measuring with *rulers* as possible; also known as free-piecing

Piece: a single bit of fabric with no seams

Unit: two or more pieces sewn together

Base: the piece or unit that you are adding fabric to

Block: a completed unit; can be a single letter or a complete word

Equalizer: the extra fabric sewn on when you "add to it"

Spacer: the bit of background fabric that goes between letters and words

Bias: the stretchy edge that results when fabric is cut on an angle rather than following the grain or weave

Wonky: an informal British term meaning "unsteady, not straight or level"; a wonderful description for UnRuly letters

Cutting Tools

Scissors: Scissors are great for snipping off the end of a fabric strip and for trimming small units. I use my scissors all the time while working at my sewing machine. My scissor cuts are always a bit crooked, which gives my letters more personality than if I slice them precisely with a rotary cutter and a ruler. The more you use your scissors, the less perfect your letters will be—and that's good.

Rotary cutter: I do prefer a rotary cutter for cutting strips and large shapes, and for making diagonal cuts.

Rulers: I often use my rectangular ruler as a straight edge, not as a measuring device. For my purposes, a long ruler—for example, 6" x 24"—is great. I use my square rulers to straighten the sides of units and for making them the same height. Square rulers are also wonderful for trimming blocks to a uniform size. I recommend the 6", 8", and 12" square rulers in particular.

You may have heard quilting "rules" such as: "Only use one ruler to do all measuring for a single project" and "Never use the cutting mat to measure." I never bother with any of that; for these quilts, I don't need precision.

Sewing Machine

Yes, please use one. (If you hand piece, you'll compromise seams when you cut through them the way you will for these letters!)

Remember when I said you can use any ruler or mat to measure? Same goes with sewing machines. Yes, sewing on different machines with different feet can give you varying seam allowances. That doesn't matter here.

Seam Allowances

By now you might have guessed that a perfect ¼" seam allowance isn't necessary for making UnRuly letters; this method isn't about exact sizes. A ¼" seam allowance is your general goal, but don't stress about it. Sew in a straight enough line that the seam allowances will press flat, and with enough allowance to stand up to use without fraying.

I tend to use a smaller stitch length for this technique—typically 14 to 15 stitches per inch. (On my machine that's a setting of 2.) With all the cutting and trimming, these smaller stitches strengthen the seams.

If you're sewing two pieces together and have a choice, put the piece with bias edges on the bottom; the feed dogs help stabilize it.

> **GREAT FOR GROUP PROJECTS!**
>
> Since it doesn't require an accurate or consistent ¼" seam allowance, UnRuly piecing is a great choice for group quilts.

Pinning, Pressing, and Ripping

For anything over 10" in length I pin about every 1½", if not more closely.

I finger-press seam allowances flat while I'm working on a small unit, but use an iron to press pieces with angles and when the unit is complete. Always press the unit open before you trim. Beware of bias edges: With all the random cuts, there will be lots of them. Don't pull at them or they will stretch. The more stretched your unit or block, the more rippled or wavy it will be.

Sometimes—for example, when I want my letters to really pop out—I press toward the letter strips, but usually I press whichever way has the fewest seams.

Think before using your seam ripper. If you sewed a unit "incorrectly," perhaps you've just discovered a new way to make a letter—or maybe a cat. Take into account the kind of quilt you're making. Is it folk art? Then a backward *N* or *S* just might be fabulous.

> **BASIC UNRULY TECHNIQUES**
>
> Here's how free-piecing works at its most basic level.
>
> **The most important rules are these:**
>
> • If it's too long, cut it off.
>
> • If it's too short, add to it.

Cut It Off

Let's look at an illustrated example of how easy it is to be free and just lop off bits that aren't needed.

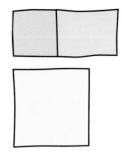

Here we'll be sewing a larger unit to a smaller base piece (in this case, a yellow square).

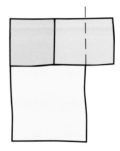

Cut off the excess with scissors, or align a ruler along the edge of the base piece and slice with a rotary cutter.

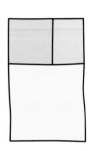

Either way you end up with a straight edge.

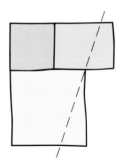

Rather not follow the base piece? You don't have to. Add wonkiness by cutting at an angle.

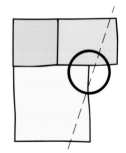

Just don't leave any gaps!

Even when you're not working with squares and rectangles—for example, when you're sewing a strip to a triangle—the process works exactly the same way.

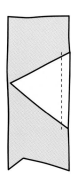

Here the triangle is the base piece.

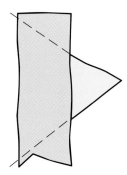

When sewing a triangle to a strip, center the edge of the triangle on the strip so that plenty of strip fabric extends beyond the triangle on both sides. The wider the strip, the more overhang you'll need on either side of the triangle.

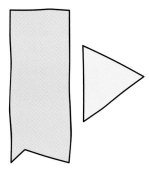

After sewing, press open and follow the edges of the triangle to trim.

Add It On

Sometimes you need a unit to be bigger, not smaller.

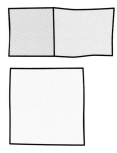

Suppose the top unit needs to stay the length it is, but the unit you are stitching it to isn't long enough?

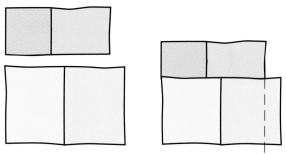

Easy! Add a piece to the smaller unit, then join the units and trim if needed.

STRIP VERSATILITY

Take advantage of the *length* of your strips, not just the width. You can stitch the *edge* of a strip *or* the *end* of a strip to the base piece.

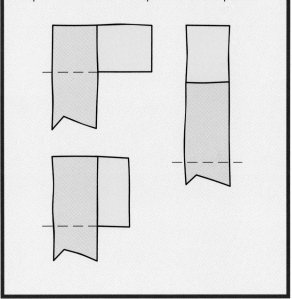

Joining Angles

With UnRuly piecing (as well as traditional piecing), any time you have an angle, you must offset the pieces to account for the width of the seam allowance.

The previous example showed how to join 45° angles—the kind often used to join strips for binding. When the angle is *less* than 45°, you still need to offset, but not as dramatically. With free-piecing, it's (usually) not a big deal if you get this wrong, as you can just trim off any excess.

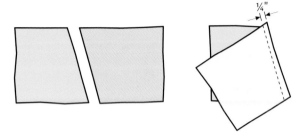

Place the pieces right sides together and offset so that the two meet ¼" from the edge.

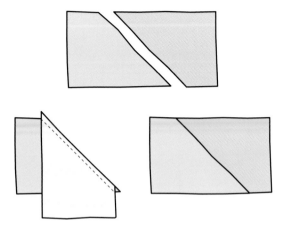

To join two angled pieces or strips, place right sides together with the pointy bits sticking out. Start sewing ¼" from the edge, at the spot where the two pieces meet.

To sum up, when joining angles—whether 45° degrees or otherwise—offset. You'll use this technique a lot.

Inserting Strips

Inserting a strip means cutting through a base fabric (or unit) and sewing a strip into the gap. In the following examples, the square is the base.

One of the joys of free-piecing is its adaptability. Sometimes, if you didn't offset pieces, you can simply cut off the excess bits. You'll end up with a narrower unit, but that only matters if it *had* to be a certain width. Note, however, that cutting off excess width doesn't work so well if you're joining long strips. In that case you'll need the seam ripper.

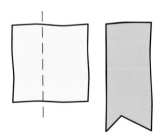

Slice the base so that the strip can be inserted.

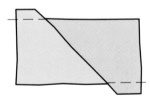

Trim excess to make a straight edge.

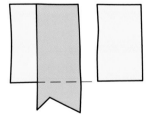

Flip the strip over to place it right sides together with one piece of the base; stitch, press open, and trim. Add the remaining base piece.

Inserting a strip at an angle is slightly trickier . . . but only slightly. You're joining angles, so don't forget to offset!

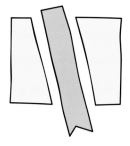 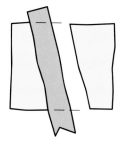

Slice the base at a rough diagonal—not exactly into either corner—and place the strip in the gap.

Place the strip and one base piece right sides together, offset by ¼", and sew. Press open and trim. Add the remaining base piece.

Inserting a Strip into a Corner

This time, you're going to insert the strip right into the corner. Inserting a strip at a corner is really useful for making the letter X. In the examples shown, the square is the base.

Slice the base from corner to corner so that the strip can be inserted.

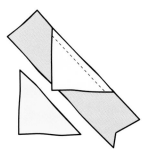 

Leaving extra length at both ends of the strip, flip one triangle, right sides together, onto the strip. Stitch and press open.

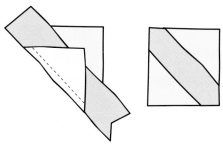

Add the other base triangle. To maintain the square shape, align the next base bit as shown. Stitch, press open, and trim.

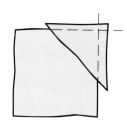 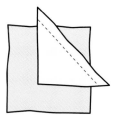

Another option is to align the second base triangle differently so you end up with a rectangle.

Adding Corner Triangles

You can give your letters a rounder appearance by adding triangles to the corners. I do this when I make a capital *D*, for example, as you'll see on page 22.

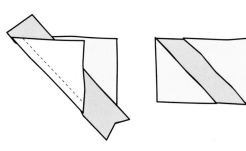

Place an oversized half-square triangle right sides together on the corner of your base piece. The triangle points should stick out *at least* ¼" as shown. Sew the triangle to the base.

Press the triangle open and trim the excess fabric even with the corner. Trim the base fabric beneath the triangle, leaving a ¼" seam allowance.

Duplicating an Angle

Remember what I said about bias being stretchy? If you use my method for duplicating angles, you can avoid having so much bias on the edges of your blocks. This technique really comes in handy for the letter V and a slanted capital A.

Suppose you have a triangle that needs to be turned into a square or rectangle. You could sew the edge of the triangle to a rectangle or strip, and square off the edges. The downside is all the stretchy bias you get on the edge of the letter unit.

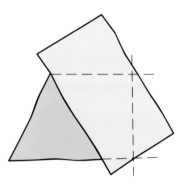

Here's how to duplicate an angle to avoid bias on the edges of your letters and blocks.

1. With both pieces facing up, place the base (A) on a wide strip or rectangle of fabric (B). Position A so that B extends *at least* ½" taller and ½" wider than the angled edge you wish to duplicate. The narrower and steeper the triangle, the more extra you'll need. Use your ruler and rotary cutter to slice B along the edge of A. It's OK if you cut into A somewhat, since the goal is to have the angles match. By cutting this way, they will.

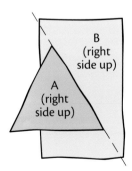

2. Flip the new B triangle onto your base, right sides together, and sew. Press and trim as shown. Notice that the cuts follow two sides of A.

3. Using another wide strip or rectangle (B), repeat steps 1 and 2 to add the other side of the unit as shown.

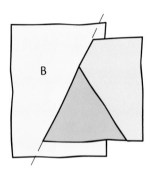

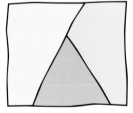

MAKING LETTERS AND NUMBERS

These instructions are for making the specific characters. If you're not sure
of a technique, refer to "UnRuly Letter Basics" (page 13).

Preparing Strips

I suggest that you cut only one strip of each
fabric at first and then cut more as needed. Cut
additional strips at different widths if you'd like,
perhaps angling some for wonkiness.

Generally speaking, you will need two different
widths of strips for letters (or numbers) and three
to four widths of strips for background. Listed
below are the widths I typically use; these strips will
yield small characters that finish at approximately
3½" tall, which is the size I prefer. You can use my
measurements, but feel free to make these "-ish"
widths. If you want bigger letters, add ½" or 1" to
each measurement. For now, I recommend that
you make the letters and numbers individually,
and hold off on adding spacers and background
around them. We'll get to that later.

Cut letter strips:
> narrow—1" wide
> medium—1½" wide

Cut background strips:
> narrow—1" wide
> medium—1½" wide
> wide—2" wide
> widest—3" wide*

Used rarely and only in angled sections.

Piecing the Letters

We'll start with the easy letters and build on them.
(That's why letters do not appear in alphabetical
order.) Once you're familiar with the methods,
there's an alphabetized chart of capital and
lowercase letters, followed by numbers, beginning
on page 62, for easy reference.

**"NOEL,"
19½" x 22½", 2005,
designed, made,
and hand quilted
by the author. This
quilt is an example
of an alphabet
sampler. You'll
learn more about
samplers beginning
on page 49.**

You don't need to make all the letters if you don't want to, but I do recommend that you read the instructions and understand the process.

Each illustration includes numbers to indicate the piecing order; a number may appear twice if it doesn't matter which piece or strip is sewn first. When letters or numbers are constructed in separate sections, one unit is numbered in the proper sewing order and the other unit is alphabetical.

When I say "cut a square/rectangle," just cut the segment from the end of a strip with your scissors. There's no need to make it perfect. If you cut it at a bit of an angle or if it's a "rectangly" square, that's fine. If no specific strip width is given, choose whatever proportions look best to you.

The letters shown here were intentionally left a bit generic to make it easier to learn the technique. Once you're familiar with the techniques, you'll be throwing in your own twists, making letters asymmetrical or adding more angles.

Capital Letters

We'll start with the easiest of the capital letters, and go from there. Remember: the key is to have fun!

Capital *T* and *I*

1. To make capital *T*, cut a rectangle from a medium letter strip. Sew it lengthwise to a background strip; press and trim.

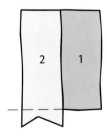

2. Sew the unit lengthwise to another background strip; press and trim.

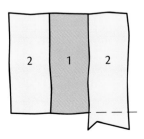

3. Sew a letter strip to the top of the unit; press and trim.

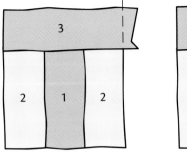

4. To make capital *I*, repeat steps 1–3, this time beginning with a shorter rectangle or a square letter strip. Add a letter strip at the bottom; press and trim.

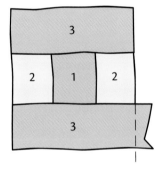

Capital *H*

Capital *H* can be made in the same manner as *I*—just turned on its side.

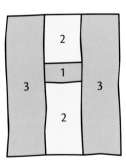

Another option is to use strip insertion. Cut a background strip into a rectangle *at least* 2½" long. Referring to "Inserting Strips" (page 16), insert a narrow letter strip at an angle. Sew letter strips to the sides; press and trim.

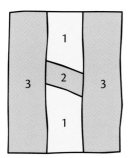

Capital *L, U, C,* and **O**

1. For capital *L*, cut a rectangle (or square) from a wide background strip, and sew it to the edge of a letter strip; press and trim.

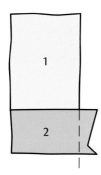

2. Sew a letter strip to the left edge of the unit from step 1; press and trim.

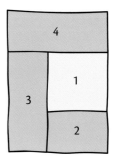

3. Capital *U* is made pretty much like an *L*, but with another strip of letter fabric added to its right edge.

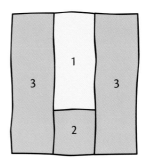

4. To make capital C, repeat steps 1 and 2, this time beginning with a square cut from a wide background strip. Sew a letter strip to the top; press and trim.

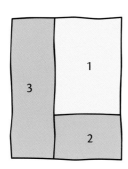

5. Now that you've made C, I know you can figure out how to make capital O!

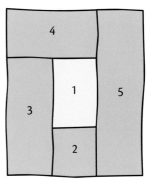

Capital **D**

This is the easiest way to make capital *D* and one that I'd never thought of—it's a marvelous student invention.

1. Make a capital *O* (page 21).

2. Cut a square from a medium (or wide) background strip, and divide it diagonally from corner to corner.

3. Add corner triangles to the right top and bottom corners of the *O*. Can't remember how? Go back to "Adding Corner Triangles" (page 17).

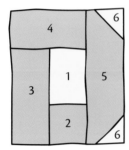

Capital **Q**

The letter *Q* can be made in several different ways, some of which are time-consuming and fiddly. To save the stress, here's an easy method. If you still want to try something more complicated, I suggest waiting until you have a bit more experience piecing the letters.

1. Make a capital *O* (page 21).

2. Cut a square of narrow letter fabric and sew it to the end of a narrow background strip; press and trim.

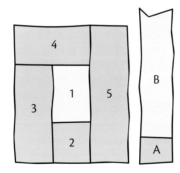

3. Sew the unit from step 2 to the right edge of the *O*; press and trim.

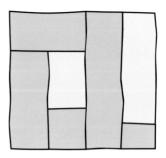

Capital **P**

1. Cut a square of narrow background fabric and sew it to a narrow letter strip; press and trim. Sew medium letter strips to the right and top edges of the unit, pressing and trimming after adding each strip. Your unit should look like a backward *C*.

2. Sew a wide background strip to the bottom of the unit; press and trim.

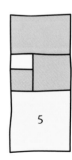

3. Sew a letter strip to the left side of the unit; press and trim.

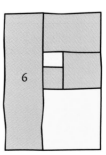

Capital **F** and **E**

1. To make capital *F*, cut a rectangle from a medium letter strip, and sew it to the edge of a narrow background strip; press and trim. Sew a narrow letter strip to the bottom of the unit; press and trim.

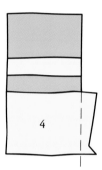

2. Sew a wide background strip to the bottom of the unit; press and trim.

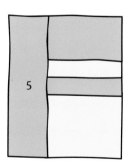

3. Sew a medium letter strip to the left edge of the unit; press and trim.

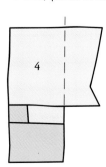

4. To make capital *E*, repeat step 1. Sew a narrow background strip and then a letter strip to the bottom of the unit, pressing and trimming after adding each strip.

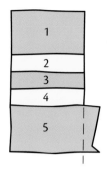

5. Sew a medium letter strip to the left edge of the unit; press and trim.

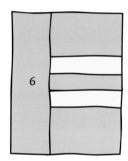

Capital **J**

1. Cut a square from a narrow letter strip. Sew the square to a medium background strip; press and trim. Sew a medium letter strip to the bottom edge as shown; press and trim.

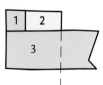

2. Sew a wide (or widest) background strip to the top edge of the unit; press and trim.

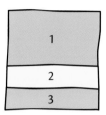

3. Sew a letter strip to the right edge of the unit; press and trim.

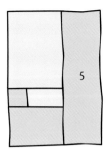

Capital G

Pay attention while you're making the G—it's easy to sew something in the wrong place!

1. Cut one square each from a narrow letter strip and a narrow background strip. Sew the squares together; press. Sew a narrow background strip to the bottom of the unit, making sure to orient the squares as shown; press and trim.

2. Sew a medium letter strip to the right edge of the unit; press and trim. Sew a narrow background strip to the top edge; press and trim.

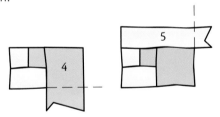

3. You've gotten this far; the worst is over. Sew medium letter strips to the bottom, left, and top edges, pressing and trimming after adding each strip. There you go!

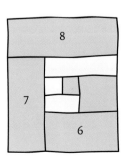

Capital B

Capital B isn't hard to make; it just takes several steps. You need to make two different units and then join them before the final piece is added. For easy reference, I've used numbers to label the top unit and letters for the bottom.

1. Start with the top unit. Cut a square from a narrow background strip and sew it to the left edge of a medium letter strip; press and trim.

2. Sew a narrow letter strip to the top edge of the unit; press and trim.

3. Sew a narrow background strip to the right edge of the unit; press and trim to complete the top unit.

4. The bottom unit is easier. Cut a square from a medium background strip. Sew letter strips to the right, bottom, and top edges, pressing and trimming after adding each strip.

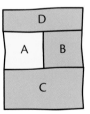

5. Sew the top and bottom units together as shown; press and trim. Sew a letter strip to the left edge; press and trim.

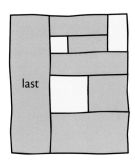

Capital *S*

Like *B*, capital *S* is made in two separate sections. Here's what works for me.

1. Cut one rectangle each from a narrow letter strip and a medium letter strip. Sew both pieces lengthwise to a narrow background strip; press and trim as shown.

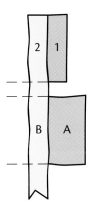

2. Sew the units to a medium letter strip with the background strips facing each other as shown; press and trim.

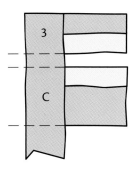

3. Rotate the units as shown. Sew the units together; press. Sew a medium letter strip to the bottom edge; press and trim.

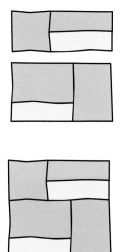

SOMETHING NOT QUITE RIGHT?

If your units look like those shown below, then you've sewn the letter fabric strips to the wrong side of the units, and you're making a number 2 rather than an S.

If you're making a folk-arty, fun, wonky quilt, go ahead and use that backward S. Lots of antique quilts have backward letters—they add charm!

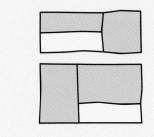

Capital Letters with Angles

This is where we begin working with angles to make letters.

Capital **X**

If you want the finished X to be a square (rather than a rectangle as shown here), start with a square of background fabric and use letter strips of matching width.

1. Cut a rectangle from the *widest* background strip, and divide it diagonally from corner to corner. This is your base.

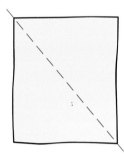

2. Referring to "Inserting Strips" (page 16), insert a letter strip into the base; press and trim. **Note:** If you're using two different widths of letter strips, insert the wide one first, or else the final X will be mismatched.

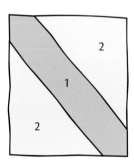

3. Slice the unit diagonally from corner to corner in the opposite direction.

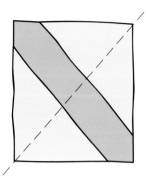

4. Sew a letter strip, offsetting it a bit, onto one cut edge of the unit; press and trim. Line up the other side of the X by matching the two ends of the first letter strip. Sew, press, and trim.

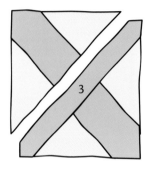 

Capital **N** and **Z**

1. To make capital N, cut a rectangle from a medium background strip. I've discovered that the base rectangle needs to be 1" longer than I want the finished N to be. Starting with a $4\frac{1}{2}$" rectangle and inserting a 1" strip gives you a letter that finishes $3\frac{1}{2}$", more or less.

2. Slice the rectangle diagonally from $\frac{1}{2}$" beneath the upper-left corner to $\frac{1}{2}$" (or higher) above the lower-right corner.

3. Referring to "Inserting Strips" (page 16), insert a letter strip into the base; press and trim. This will be the unfinished height of the letter. If you want a taller letter, sew a strip of background fabric to the bottom edge.

4. Add letter strips to opposite sides of the unit; press and trim.

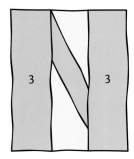

5. Capital Z is basically an *N* tipped on its side. This time, start with a rectangle cut from a wide background strip. Turn the rectangle as shown, and slice it diagonally ¼" from the lower-left corner to ¼" from the upper-right corner.

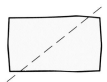

6. Referring to "Inserting Strips," insert a letter strip into the base from step 5; press and trim. Sew medium letter strips to the top and bottom; press and trim.

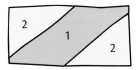

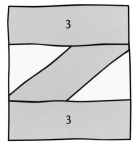

Capital **R**

Capital R is constructed in two units, with the top unit made like a capital *P*. You simply add an angled leg.

1. Refer to step 1 of "Capital *P*" (page 22) to construct the top unit.

2. From a wide background strip, cut a rectangle about ¼" longer than the top unit. Turn the rectangle as shown, and slice it diagonally a scant ½" from the upper-left corner to a scant ½" from the lower-right corner. Referring to "Inserting Strips" (page 16), insert a letter strip; press and trim.

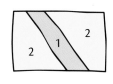

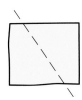

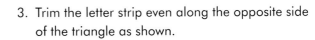

3. Sew the top and bottom units together as shown; press and trim. Sew a letter strip to the left edge; press and trim.

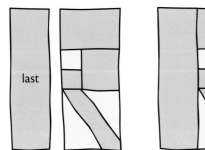

Capital V

1. Cut a long rectangle from a medium (or wide) background strip. Cut the background piece into an elongated triangle. The point doesn't need to be in the middle.

2. Sew a letter strip to the elongated triangle, offsetting the top of the strip as shown; press and trim evenly across the top of the triangle. **Optional:** To make the V a certain height, measure from the top of the unit, and make a second cut parallel to the first.

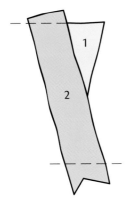

3. Trim the letter strip even along the opposite side of the triangle as shown.

4. Use the same method to sew a letter strip to the opposite side of the unit; press and trim.

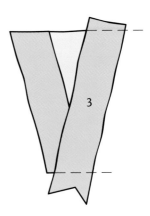

5. From a wide (or widest) background strip, cut a rectangle approximately ½" taller than the unit from step 4. (If you're nervous, cut a larger rectangle. It's easy to cut off what you don't need.) Refer to "Duplicating an Angle" (page 18) and cut the background angle for the left edge of the unit.

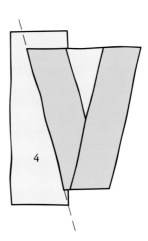

6. Offset and sew the trimmed background piece to the left edge of the unit. Press, and then trim the strip even with the unit on the top and bottom edges. Leave any excess at the side outer edge for now.

7. Repeat steps 5 and 6 to sew a background piece to the right edge of the unit; press and trim. Leave a good ¼" on either side of the V on top, or you'll lose part of the letter when you sew the seam allowances. If you leave even more than that, you might not need to add spacers on the sides when you join it to other letters. This rule holds true for the slanted capital A (below) and slanted W (page 30) as well.

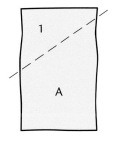

Capital **A**

The easiest way to make a capital A is to make a capital H (page 20) with a strip of letter fabric across the top. Boom, done. Suppose, however, you want a slanted A. That's easy too. It's just an upside-down capital V with a letter strip inserted across the center.

1. Refer to step 1 of "Capital V" to cut an elongated triangle from a background strip as instructed. Slice the triangle crosswise. Referring to "Inserting Strips" (page 16), insert a narrow letter strip; press and trim.

2. Refer to "Capital V", steps 2–7, to complete the slanted A.

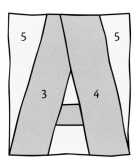

Capital **K**

This letter K is made in two parts.

1. From your widest background strip, cut a rectangle approximately 1" taller than you want the finished letter to be. Turn the rectangle as shown, and divide it by cutting from the middle of the left edge to a scant ½" below the upper-right corner. Sew a narrow letter strip (2) to the bottom edge of the upper piece (1); press and trim.

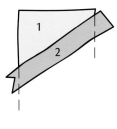

2. Divide the bottom piece (A) approximately as shown. (It doesn't need to be exact.) Referring to "Inserting Strips" (page 16), insert a narrow letter strip; press and trim.

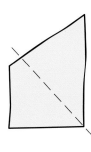
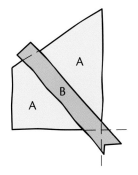

3. Sew the units from steps 1 and 2 together as shown; press and trim. Sew a letter strip to the left edge of the unit; press and trim.

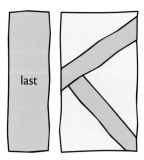

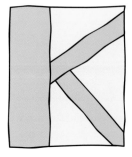

Capital **M**

The easy M is a capital E (page 23) knocked on its side so that it is face down. Here is an alternate version that uses a small V at its center.

1. Cut a square from a wide background strip, and cut it to make an elongated triangle as shown.

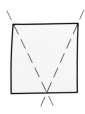

2. Refer to "Capital V," steps 2–7 (page 28), and make a V. You can offset the angle just a bit when you add the narrow letter strip, but it doesn't need to be much. The legs finish more on the sides of the unit rather than completely on top as in a real V.

3. Sew a wide background strip to the bottom of the unit from step 2; trim and press.

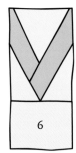

4. Sew a letter strip to the left and right edges of the unit; press and trim.

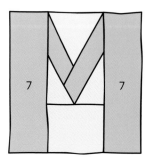

Capital **W**

The easy W is a capital E (page 23) tipped on its side, this time face up . . . or you can turn a capital M (at left) upside down. It's possible, however, to angle the legs so that the letter looks more W-like.

1. Repeat the process for making the center section of capital M, but angle the legs of the V straight into the corners. Rotate the unit as shown, and sew a wide background strip to the top edge, overlapping the ends of the strip a bit on both sides; press and trim as shown.

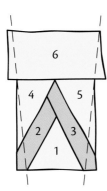

2. Sew a letter strip to both sides of the unit; press and trim. Refer to "Duplicating an Angle" (page 18), and sew background fabric to each side; press and trim.

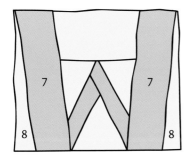

Capital Y

This is another letter that is made as two units. This time we'll make the bottom unit first.

1. Cut a rectangle from a medium letter strip. Sew wide background strips to opposite sides; press and trim the top and bottom edges. (The unit will be wider than needed for now.)

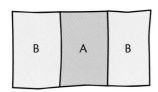

2. Once again, you'll make the top unit as a small V. Cut a square from a wide background strip, and cut it to make a triangle as shown.

3. Refer to "Capital V," steps 2–4 (page 28), and sew medium letter strips to the sides of the triangle to make a V. The bottom doesn't need to be pointy.

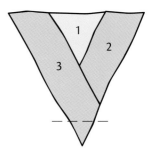

4. Refer to "Duplicating an Angle" (page 18), and cut and sew the background triangles for the left edge and then the right edge of the unit; press and trim.

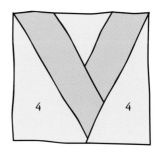

5. Depending on how well you want the top and bottom units to match up, you'll need to fiddle a bit. Trim the bottom edge of the top unit so that the blunt end of the V measures approximately ¼" less than the A peace in the bottom section,

and line up the bottom unit when you turn the units right sides together to sew them. After you've sewn the top and bottom units together, you can press and trim the excess.

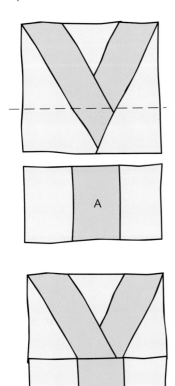

Lowercase Letters

Lowercase letters are generally even easier to make than the capitals. Quite a few are made the same way as their capital counterparts, although you may wish to make them smaller. For example, lowercase *c*, *o*, *p*, *s*, *u*, *v*, *x*, and *z* are constructed the same way as the capitals. I'm guessing you can figure out how to make an *l*.

Little *k* is the same as capital K (page 29), but I make the V section smaller, using only narrow letter strips. I then sew background fabric across the top of the unit before adding the letter fabric along the left side.

Lowercase *d* is just a *p* turned upside down. Little *b* is *d*, just backwards.

You'll find these "missing" letters in the chart that begins on page 62; the others follow. Once again we start with the easiest letters.

Lowercase *i* and *j*

I'm not really going to tell you how to make an *i*. You can make this super-easy letter using strip insertion (see "Inserting Strips" on page 16) or by starting with a square of letter fabric.

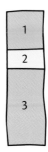

The *j* is made in two simple units, one of which is an *i*. If you want the fancy curl at the end, look at capital J (page 23). Use a lowercase *i* to replace section 5 in the capital J.

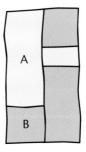

Lowercase *h* and *y*

1. To make *h*, cut a square from a medium letter strip, and sew it to the right edge of a narrow background strip; press and trim. Sew a narrow letter strip to the top; press and trim.

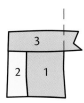

2. Sew the top edge of the unit to the end of a wide background strip. That way you can press and then trim the letter to make it as tall as you want it to be. Sew a letter strip to the left edge; press and trim.

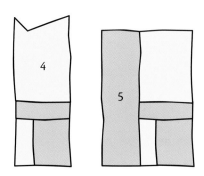

3. The *y* is just a shortened *h* turned upside down with a medium letter strip added to the bottom.

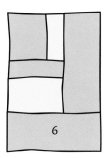

Lowercase *t* and *f*

1. The easiest way to make a *t* is to insert a strip for the crossbar. Piece a rectangle cut from a letter strip between two background strips; press and trim. Slice the unit crosswise, and insert a strip of narrow letter fabric; press and trim. Refer back to "Inserting Strips" (page 16) for guidance if needed.

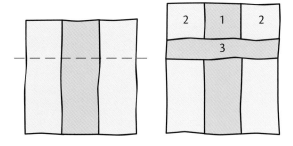

PLAYING WITH ANGLES

If you slice the unit at an angle, you can insert the crossbar at a jaunty angle to make a more interesting letter. See my quilt "Vote" (page 59) for an example.

2. The *f* is just a *t*, with a medium letter strip sewn to the top edge of the right-side background strip. Once you have that, just follow step 1 to complete the letter.

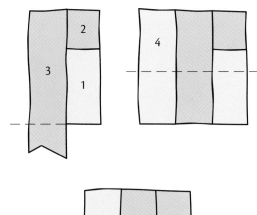

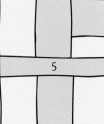

Lowercase **e** and **a**

1. The easiest way to make a lowercase *e* is to make a capital *P* (page 22), replacing the wide background strip in step 2 (5) with a narrow background strip. Finish by adding a medium letter strip to the bottom edge of the unit; press and trim.

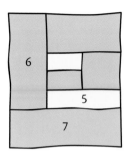

2. Lowercase *a* is easy; just turn *e* upside down.

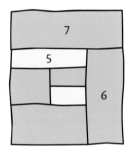

Lowercase **q** and **g**

1. Lowercase q is the same as capital *P*, just backwards. If you wish, you could add a tail in a similar fashion to capital *Q* (page 22). By the way, you'll notice that the tailless *q* also makes the number *9*.

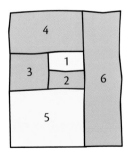

2. The lowercase *g* is made pretty much like *q*; simply replace the wide background strip (5) with a narrow background strip. Finish by adding a medium letter strip to the bottom edge of the unit; press and trim. Turn it upside down and you've got the number *6*.

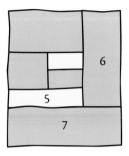

Lowercase **r, n, m,** and **w**

1. To make *r*, refer to "Inserting Strips" (page 16), and insert an angled letter strip into a wide background strip; press and trim to the desired height. Sew a medium letter strip to the left edge of the unit; press and trim.

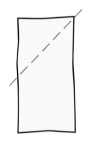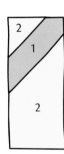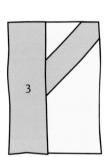

2. A lowercase *n* is simply a skinny *r* with an extra letter strip sewn to its right edge.

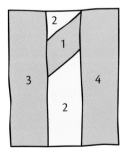

3. You can make a super-easy *m* by constructing a smaller version of capital *E* (page 23) and knocking it over on its side. An alternate version, shown here, is very similar to *n*, but with an additional unit sewn to its right edge. I think you can figure out how to do this!

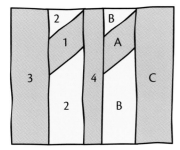

4. Lowercase *w* is just an upside-down *m*.

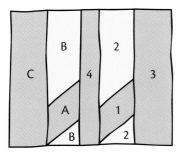

NOT TO WORRY

Don't worry if the *n* looks a little goofy; it will be easily recognizable once it's sewn into a quilt. This is true of some other letters as well, such as the lowercase *m*, *w*, and *z*.

Piecing the Numbers

Numbers are easy to make once you've done the letters.

    0 = capital *O*

    1 = lowercase *l*

    2 = capital *Z* (page 26) or backward capital *S* (page 25)

    3 = backward capital *E* (page 23)

    4 = upside-down lowercase *h* (page 33)

    5 = capital *S*

    6 = upside-down lowercase *g* (page 34)

    9 = lowercase *q* (page 34)

    The characters for *7* and *8* are a bit different, so let's look at how to make those.

Number 7

A *7* is similar to a capital *Z*, but without the bottom letter strip.

1. Cut a rectangle from the widest background strip. Turn the rectangle as shown, and slice it diagonally ¼" from the lower-left corner to ¼" from the upper-right corner.

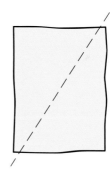

2. Referring to "Inserting Strips" (page 16), insert a medium letter strip into the base from step 1; press and trim. Sew a medium letter strip to the top; press and trim.

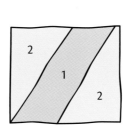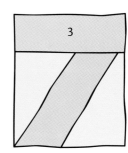

Number **8**

The number *8* is made in two units.

1. We'll start with the top. Cut a square from a narrow background strip. Sew this piece between two narrow letter strips; press and trim. Sew a medium letter strip to the top edge; press and trim.

2. Sew the unit between two narrow background strips; press and trim to complete the top unit.

3. For the bottom unit, cut a rectangle from a narrow background strip, and sew it between two medium letter strips; press and trim. Sew this unit between a narrow letter strip and a medium letter strip; press and trim to complete the bottom unit.

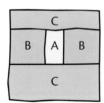

4. Sew the top and bottom units together as shown; press and trim.

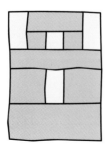

Adjusting Letter and Number Size

Now that you know how to make the letters and numbers, go, play, and have fun. If you decide you want a character to finish at a particular size, come back to the following pages for help. Although I refer to letters, the information pertains to numbers as well.

Adjusting Height

The height of a letter is determined by the levels of strips from top to bottom. For example, *O* is three strips high and *E* is five strips high. You can make those five strips any width you wish.

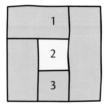

If you use extremely narrow strips, cut at ¾", your *O* will finish at ¾" tall and your capital *E* will shrink to a finished height of 1¼". That's pretty small.

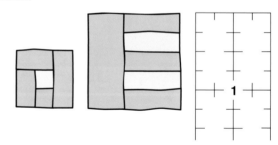

The minimum finished letter height I like to work with is 2". You have a lot of room to play at that height.

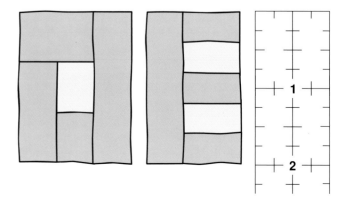

In short, you can customize a letter to any height you like by changing the width of the strips. The skinnier the strips, the smaller the letter. The reverse is also true: the wider the strips, the taller the letter . . . so if you make an *E* using all 2½" strips, it will finish at 10" tall.

Adjusting Width

The width of a letter depends on the number of strips placed side by side, as well as the width of those strips. Most letters are three strips wide; however, lowercase *i* and *l*, and the numeral *1*, are only one strip wide, and can be your thinnest characters.

Depending on how you make them, the *M*, *m*, *W*, and *w* are almost always the widest characters. The skinniest I've been able to make them is four strips wide. For an example, look at the *M* in my quilt "America with Flag" (page 42); the center of the letter is two strips wide.

You can fiddle with the width measurements, much as you did to adjust the height. *Must* your letters be a certain width? Time to get out the graph paper! More on that shortly.

TIPS FOR ADJUSTING LETTER HEIGHT

Determine the minimum height of the character by counting how many levels of strips you'll need from top to bottom. Letters to watch out for include *a*, *E*, *e*, *S*, *s*, *B*, *G*, and *g*; numbers to watch out for are *3*, *5*, *6*, and *8*. Why? Because these characters are all five strip levels tall. The number *2* may also fall in this category, depending on how you make it; *R* can be tricky too.

• Use the *narrowest* strips for the interior of the letters. For instance, the *E* has three strips in the middle (two background/one letter)—make those the skinniest. An *O* that starts with a 1" center square will be smaller (or can be cut down smaller) than one with a 2" center. This is true of more complicated letters like capital *G* and *P* as well. Use your narrowest strips for the interior pieces (1 and 2 in the diagram). That way, you can reduce the height of the letter and it will still be readable.

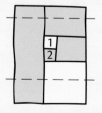

• Make the top and bottom strips much wider than you need them. This allows you to trim them to a smaller size later if necessary.

• Take full advantage of the length of your strips, sewing onto the ends rather than cutting them in advance. The same goes for inserting strips. For example, consider the center of capital *H*. Inserting the letter strip into a long, uncut background strip allows you to trim the background at any point to get a letter the height you need.

This works for letters with angles, too, such as with this *N*.

Use your imagination! A capital *K* could be made as shown. It's really hard to insert an angle in a long skinny background, but making the letter like this bypasses the need to do so.

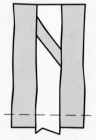

WORKING WITH WORDS

Until now, we've worked only with individual letters (and numbers), but now
we're moving on to putting those letters into words.

Figuring Word Length

If you want your word(s) to fit into an area with exact dimensions, there is a simple way to accomplish this. In the following example, the goal is to get the word *HOPE* into a 7" x 10" space.

Use a pen or pencil to draw a 7" x 10" rectangle on graph paper. Decide what strip widths you're comfortable sewing.

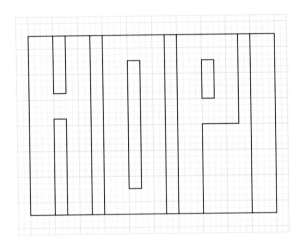

Oops! Using 1½"-wide letter strips and 1"-wide background spacers isn't going to work.

Suppose you make each letter in a different fabric for contrast and then butt one right up against another, without spacers.

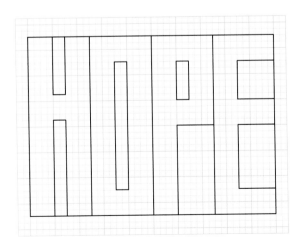

That works. The word could fit the space if you used 1½"-wide letter strips and 1"- and 2"-wide background strips.

Now, I hope you wouldn't use that graph paper to measure each bit and cut pieces to size. That's not necessary. As long as you're using strips in the widths you've determined, you're pretty safe. The only place I can see getting carried away is the background in the *E*. Watch for that and you're set.

Feeling brave? What happens if you don't measure and just sew? Maybe you'll come up with something more interesting, like the example below.

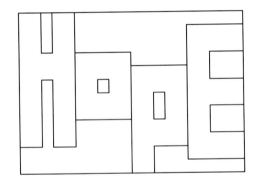

Play with the graph paper and try different strip widths until you get something that works. Once you figure out what you need, you usually don't need to measure precisely—just sew the letters by sight and see where it leads.

Assembling Words

I make all my letters before stitching any of them together. Here are the basics. **Note:** If you have fun angles that you want to keep on the outer edges of the letters, see "Letters with Angles" (page 39).

1. Trim the edges of the unfinished letters so that they are straight. They don't have to be a certain size, but they *do* need straight edges.

2. Pick an unfinished height for your word. If you have a few letters that are much taller than the rest, can you cut them down? That's one option. You can also add equalizer strips to make smaller letters taller. Be sure to trim as needed to keep the edges straight.

3. You likely will need spacers between some letters, but you may not need them between every letter. Arrange the letters for the word side by side, and look at them before you sew. Insert spacers as needed. **Note:** Watch out for the letters A, f, k, q, r, t, V, v, X, x, and Y, especially when they are next to one another. These letters often have a lot of background on one or both sides and probably won't need any more.

4. Sew the letters and spacers together to make the word, trimming again, if necessary, as you go.

TIPS FOR SPACERS

• I typically use very narrow background strips for spacers, cut ⅞" wide and finishing at about ⅜". You may prefer a wider spacer.

• I try to get into a rhythm, adding spacers only to the right sides of letters. That way I don't end up with double spacers between two letters of a word. The exception is if the left edge of the letter has an angle I want to keep; I'll put the spacer there instead.

Letters with Angles

If a letter has an angle that you'd like to maintain, you can add an extra-wide equalizer or spacer, and then trim.

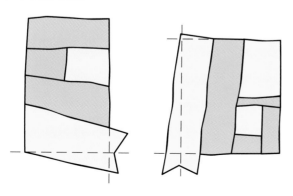

You can duplicate angles to get the same result with less bias, as described in "Duplicating an Angle" (page 18).

Making Letters "Dance"

Do you want your letters to dance up and down rather than line up in a row? If so, the letters will need some extra height. For example, the word in my quilt "Vote" (page 59) is static. The unfinished letters are 5½" tall.

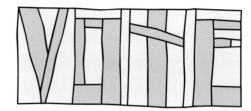

To get the same letters to dance up and down, I'd make them each 7" tall (unfinished) before joining them, using more and wider equalizer strips to make the letters jump.

To make *your* letters dance, use wider strips than you need to equalize their height. These strips can be added to the top and/or bottom of a letter and can vary in width. Once these strips are added, trim the letter to the desired unfinished height.

Notice that I didn't need to insert a spacer between the O and the *t* in this example, even though I was using just two colors.

Watch Out for Curves

Be aware that a background strip sewn to either the top or bottom of a word can cause the whole thing to develop a curve. The longer the word, the more apparent this curve may be. The example below uses a word block, but curving occurs with rows of words or letters as well. The diagram is exaggerated, but I think you get the idea. You'll be tempted to take the rotary cutter and straighten it out. Don't do it!

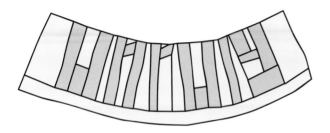

Sew the opposite seam (e.g., a background strip) before trying to straighten out the word with a ruler and rotary cutter. The seam lines, both above and below the letters, provide stability. Now you can use the rotary cutter to straighten the edges.

One-Word Quilts

A single word can be incorporated into a small wall hanging, table topper, doll quilt, place mat, pillow, tote bag, baby quilt, or whatever you'd like. Here are some ideas to get you thinking . . . and sewing.

Try This: The Priority Hope Challenge

So why did I use the word *HOPE* in a 7" x 10" space as an example on page 38?

Not too long ago, I challenged my blog readers to make a "Hope" quilt for the Alzheimer's Art Quilt Initiative (AAQI). It's a great charitable organization that requests 9" x 12" quilts to sell at auction, with the profits going to fund research into the disease. (See "Resources" on page 64 for more information.) I made the quilt "Priority Hope" (upper right) as an example.

Try making an AAQI quilt yourself. I've already given you options to make *H-O-P-E* the correct size on pages 20, 21, 22, and 23. This isn't a big investment in time or fabric, so if your first attempt doesn't come out as you wanted, try again. You'll learn plenty by doing!

Important Note: If you *do* intend to donate a quilt to AAQI, check the requirements on its website first. You'll find a lot of good information on binding and hanging small quilts there, too.

Try This: Showcase Your Fabric

I buy novelty fabric because I love it. I have no idea how I'm going to use it, but I *want* it, and then I can't bring myself to cut it up and it sits for years. That's what led me to making one-word quilts with novelty fabric, such as "Merry Penguins" (lower right).

I had a half yard of fabulous penguin fabric and didn't know what to do with it. I just knew I wanted the penguins to be the stars of a quilt. I cut the fabric in two, and took one fat quarter to play with. After straightening the edges with my rotary cutter, I had a 17" x 20" piece.

I also knew I wanted to use the word *Merry*, which so aptly describes the feeling I get looking at the fabric. The letters finish at 3½" tall and were made with strips cut in widths ranging from ⅞" to 2". I didn't prefigure the size using graph paper— I just made letters. These letters all have wide vertical pieces, so I could have trimmed ½" from each if I'd needed to.

After making the letters, I added equalizer fabric to the top of the e, which was shorter than the other characters. I then added spacers and sewed the letters all together.

The next step was to figure out how much background fabric I needed to add to the sides of the word. I cut and sewed, adding an extra inch on both edges. (I hate having things turn out too short; I prefer to trim down.) I then attached background

"PRIORITY HOPE,"
11½" x 8½", 2008,
designed, made, and
hand quilted by the
author. This is a great
example of working with
scrappy letters.

"MERRY PENGUINS,"
31" x 27½", 2007,
designed, made,
and hand quilted in
freehand fans by the
author.

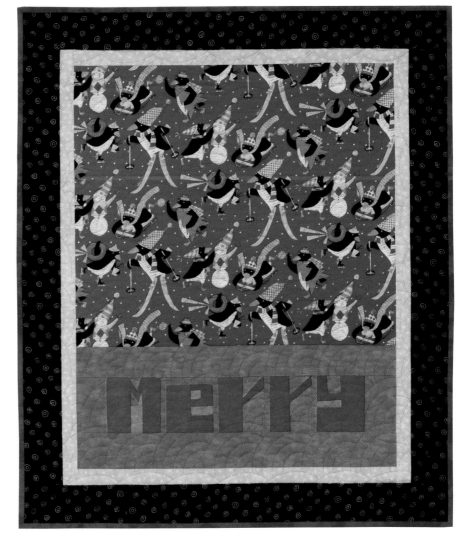

strips to the top and bottom. I picked widths I thought would look good, sewed them on, and then trimmed them even.

I centered the word beneath the fat quarter of penguin fabric. (My "precise" method was to fold both the word and the fat quarter in half and pinch, and then to match up the pinch marks.) I sewed the two together, trimmed off the excess background, and added the yellow inner border and a wide outer border.

For "America with Flag" (below), I cut ¾"- and 1"-wide strips for the letters and ¾"- and 1"-wide strips for the background, except for the background of the M, which needed a 1¼"-wide strip. The flag is made from two pieces of novelty fabric.

These letters finish about 4" high. Since the letters dance up and down, it doesn't matter if the heights are exact.

"AMERICA WITH FLAG," 15½" x 18½", 2007, designed, made, and hand quilted in wavy lines by the author.

EXPAND THE BACKGROUND

If your text is wider than your novelty print,
simply float them both within a common
background fabric, and then add a border.

"SCARY CHRISTMAS," 25" x 28", 2001, designed,
made, and hand quilted in freehand fans with pearl
cotton by the author.

Introducing Word Bricks

What else can you do with individual words? Make word bricks. I realize that "word bricks" isn't an elegant name, but it *is* descriptive. Think of how a brick house is built and you can instantly picture one way to put these word blocks together. Not every brick must have a word in it; you might substitute fun printed fabrics or solids instead.

The quilts on the next few pages should give you lots of great ideas. Then "Putting Rows Together" (page 48) gives you tips on how to accomplish them.

I made "Be Yourself" (below) as a pep talk to myself: "Be yourself. Be joyful. Be bold. . . ." I wanted to make a quilt containing every lowercase letter of the alphabet.

First, I wrote out a long list of adjectives so I'd have plenty of choices. I used a variety of hand-dyed fabrics for the backgrounds and one consistent reads-as-solid black commercial print for all the letters. I experimented, sewing super-skinny letters for *imaginative* and short letters for *creative*.

I joined the letters for each word, and then used the same fabric to surround each word that I had used to make that brick's background. I made all the blocks finish roughly the same height, knowing I could trim off extra fabric as needed when the time came to put the rows together. Before I even knew if I needed an equalizer, I added a bit of purple to the top of *colorful*, because it seemed so *uncolorful* with just turquoise and black.

I placed the bricks on my design wall and played. I had purposely split *well-loved* into

"BE YOURSELF," 48½" x 39", 2002, designed, made, and hand quilted in freehand fans with pearl cotton by the author.

separate bricks to go on different rows so that it would read as *Be well* and *Be loved*, too. Those bricks needed to be in a certain configuration; additionally, I wanted *Be* in the first slot.

I arranged and rearranged, playing with colors and brick lengths. I placed *colorful* to show off that thin wedge of purple; I didn't want it blending into another purple block. Once I was satisfied, I trimmed the bricks in each row down to the height of the shortest word, and then sewed them together to make the rows.

After sewing the bricks into rows, I added equalizers at one end or the other to make all rows the same length. The diagram below shows where I needed equalizers to fit the quilt together.

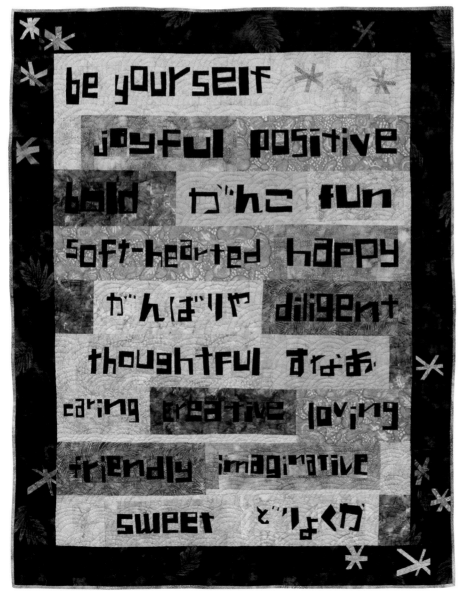

"LEIYA'S WONKY WORD," 47" x 61", 2007, designed, made, and hand quilted in freehand fans by Tanya Watanabe. Tanya made this quilt for her daughter, incorporating Japanese as well as English words. Amazingly, this was only her first UnRuly letter quilt. She'd previously experimented by making letters for place mats.

In "Four Letter Words" (below), Kathie Boucher composed all the backgrounds from different off-white and beige fabrics with words printed on them. She made the letters from contrasting solid colors, which she kept consistent within each brick. The only exceptions are the *LOVE* blocks, which I'd made and sent to her as a challenge. When all the blocks have the same or very similar backgrounds, the bricks disappear and the words really stand out.

Kathie formatted her quilt in vertical rows. The diagram below roughly shows the bricks and equalizers.

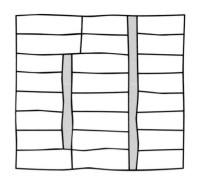

"FOUR LETTER WORDS," 65" x 52", 2009, designed, made, and machine quilted by **Kathie Enright Boucher.**

I asked readers of my blog to collaborate with me by making 12½" x 6½" bricks of happy, positive words. It was OK if the bricks weren't the perfect size, because I knew how to make them work together. (Now you do too.) The result was the quilt "Cake" (below).

Didn't these quilters make great blocks? Look at the different ways they've figured out how to make the letters. My friend Siobhan made the supersized *Cake* block (a subliminal indication of just how much she loves cake?) that wouldn't easily fit. I set that one aside and realized I had the exact number of blocks to make a square quilt.

I thought all the blocks were the same length, but it didn't quite turn out that way, so there are a few equalizers included.

The setting shown in the diagram below would have been even easier because it would automatically have an equalizer on one end of each row. The bricks could differ in length a bit and still go together smoothly.

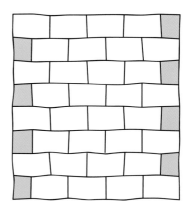

"CAKE," approximately 64" x 64", 2010, blocks made by John Adams, Chris Balchunas, Laura Banks, Kim Brandt, Sue Brown, Mary Coleman, Chris Daly, Jen Dessert, Siobhan Furgurson, Karen Griska, Nancy Hardee, Sara Homeyer, Erin Klein, Sharon Konvalin, Rondi Leslie, Cherie Moore, Belinda Noel, Annie Olson, Juliann Phillips, Julie Post, Kathy Roslasky, Julie Sefton, Cher Smith, Judy Stone, Rachael Thomas, Lynne Tyler, and Kathy Watt. Assembled by the author and quilted on a long-arm machine by Natalie Carlton.

Putting Rows Together

Here are some suggestions to help you when it's time to put rows of word bricks together. If you have rows that aren't the same length or height, either trim down or add on.

Incorporate equalizer strips at the beginnings and ends of rows, if needed, to make them long enough. You can also add strips of background fabric above and/or below the row to make it the appropriate height.

Don't worry if the corners of the blocks don't match up—the letters are UnRuly, so the quilt becomes more interesting if the blocks are too.

Be flexible. If it turns out you've mismeasured some of your rows, use your UnRuly piecing skills and keep going.

"Measure all the rows and trim them to the same length before sewing them together." That's the way you *should* do it. I'll admit: I just kind of wing it and sew the rows together first. The trick is always to have an equalizer at the end of the longer row that can be chopped off as needed.

I actually have measured two rows (or sections) of a quilt and been *convinced* that they were the same length, only to discover—as I got near the end of sewing them together—that they weren't. In a case like that, I stop sewing about 5" before the end of the seam, backstitch, and cut the thread. I then fold back the longer row and sew a strip (wider than I think I'll need) to the end of the shorter row.

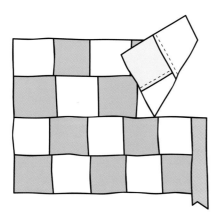

I go back to where I left off sewing the two rows together, backstitch to secure the new seam, and finish off the join. I cut off the excess, and—voilà!—it all fits together. This method works in other situations too, such as if you're running short on binding.

Thoughts on Quilting

I love the look of unmarked or casually marked quilting on these quilts. My favorite is freehand fans, which I hand quilt without marking. When a design requires that I do mark, I use chalk and mark only a small portion of the quilt at a time. I enjoy using thicker thread and larger stitches, which lend an informal, folk-art appearance. I use size 8 pearl cotton and a larger needle, such as a size 7 or 8 Between.

ALPHABET SAMPLERS

A sampler is a great way to practice *all* the letters within a single project.
You can even combine alphabets and word bricks in the same quilt.

Assemble letters for sampler quilts the same way you do for word bricks. In this case, your "word" is, for example, *ABCDEF*. For "Alphabet Sampler" (below), I used a gorgeous hand-dyed fabric that I had never worked up the nerve to cut. This fabric had the advantage, as did the solid black, of being reversible, so I could use either side.

I cut just a few strips of fabric and got started. If you look at the letters, there isn't much variety in the width of the strips.

I started at *A* and worked my way through the alphabet. (In classic do-as-I-say-not-as-I-do fashion, I recommend sewing the easiest letters first!) I used every letter and number that I made, even when I wasn't thrilled with the results. I made the letters without worrying about size and without adding any equalizers around them. I ended up with a height variance of about 2".

After I had pieced all the letters and the numbers, I moved them around over and over again to figure out how many to put in a row. I placed the numeral 0 at the end of the alphabet, simply because that worked best for making the top four rows close to the same length. I split my last name onto two lines just because I liked how it looked.

Once everything was in place, I figured out the best height for the characters in each row. I trimmed some down and added equalizers to other letters in the row to get them all the same height.

There isn't a huge height difference between one row and another—I was dealing with eighths of an inch. The variable heights added character, but took more time. I think it was worth it. Now when I'm working on a sampler quilt, I just pick one height for all the units in the quilt and adjust accordingly.

Are you ready to try a sampler of your own? Browse through the rest of the section for inspiration.

"ALPHABET SAMPLER," 36" x 38", 2000, designed, made, and hand quilted in freehand fans with pearl cotton by the author.

"LETTERS FROM HOME," 44½" x 62", 2009, designed and made by Lynne Tyler. Machine quilted by Chris Ballard.

Lynne wanted a "cheat sheet" to hang in her studio so she could look up and see how to make each letter. She took her inspiration for this quilt from New England needlework samplers, which often included a house. She designed all the blocks herself and free-pieced most of them. The capital letters at the top of the quilt finish 3" tall.

"HANGAR TALK," 57¾" x 69¾", 2008, designed, made, and hand quilted by Holly Giffin. The center of the quilt comes from a 1930s pattern called Lindy as printed in *America's Heritage Quilts* (see "Resources" on page 64).

Holly made "Hangar Talk" as a reminder of her school years in Malaysia, where she traveled back and forth to boarding school. In the quilt border, she spelled out the phonetic alphabet used by pilots. The words finish 2½" tall.

"AND SOMETIMES Y," 51" x 51", 2007, designed and made by Julie Sefton. Machine quilted by Chris Ballard.

To practice and repeat a set of letters, Julie Sefton chose *A-E-I-O-U* for this quilt. The blocks finish 5½" tall, more or less. After piecing the center, Julie decided the border needed the letter *Y*—hence the quilt's name. She used leftover letter strips to make the piano-key borders, cutting different-width strips into rectangles of the same length and sewing them into pairs, then fours, and so on until she'd made the borders the proper length.

The reverse side of "And Sometimes Y." Julie used leftover vowels and added a couple consonants to "sign" her name.

SIMPLE PROJECTS WITH IMPACT

The joy of UnRuly letters is that they are so flexible. This makes it difficult to say exactly what the outcome of any particular project will be. How I interpret the directions, how wide I choose to cut spacer and equalizer strips, and the exact sizes of my letters may be different from your interpretation, your choices, and your results. Remember: This is an improvisational way of working. Take these directions as a starting point, but feel free to adapt them however you wish.

Fat quarters are great for these little projects. Cut strips for letters and backgrounds from the longer side of the fabric (approximately 20"). Cut one strip of each given width; as you need more, cut another. Refer to "Making Letters and Numbers" (page 19) if you need help.

"CHRISTMAS JOY," 23" x 14½", 2009, designed, made, and hand quilted by the author.

Materials

Yardages given are based on a quilt that finishes the approximate size of the sample and—with the exception of fat quarters—are based on fabric that measures approximately 40" wide.

⅓ yard of fabric for border

Fat quarter *each* of 2 contrasting fabrics for letters and background (including equalizers and spacers)

⅔ yard of fabric for backing

Fat quarter for binding

29" x 20" piece of batting

Cutting

Cutting strips in the dimensions listed will yield a word that finishes approximately 4" tall as shown in the sample quilt. Change the strip widths or lengths if you like; this word is easy to enlarge so long as you are consistent with the enlargements. Changing strip measurements will change the size of the word, so adjust yardage for borders and backing and the size of the batting accordingly. Cut additional letter and background strips if needed.

From the background fabric, cut:
  1 narrow strip, 1" wide
  2 medium strips, 1½" wide
  1 wide strip, 2" wide

From the letter fabric, cut:
    1 narrow strip, 1" wide
    1 wide strip, 2" wide

From the border fabric, cut:
    2 strips, 4½" x 40"

From the backing fabric, cut:
    1 piece, 29" x 20"

From the binding fabric, cut:
    5 strips, 1½" x 20"*

For single-fold binding that finishes approximately ⅜" wide.

Making the Quilt Top

Refer to "UnRuly Letter Basics" (page 13) and "Working with Words" (page 38) as needed.

1. Beginning with a square cut from the wide background strip, make a capital O (page 21). Use narrow letter strips for the top and left edges, and wide letter strips for the bottom and right edges.

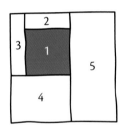

2. Beginning with a square cut from the wide background fabric, make a lowercase y. This y is pieced in a slightly different order than the one shown on page 33, and the strip proportions vary a bit too, but the basic techniques apply.

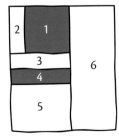

3. The J in this quilt is a little bit different from the one I showed you in "Capital J" (page 23). Cut a square from the narrow letter strip. Sew the square onto the end of the narrow background strip, *but don't trim.* Sew the unit to a square cut from the wide background strip and then trim even as shown.

4. Sew a wide letter strip to the bottom edge of the unit from step 3; press and trim. Sew a wide letter strip and then a narrow background strip along the right edge, pressing and trimming after adding each strip. Sew a narrow letter strip to the top; press and trim.

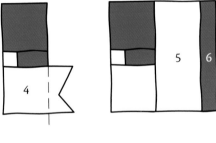

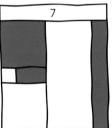

5. Add background equalizer strips (for example, to the top of the O) so that all the letter units are the same height. Press, and trim as needed.

6. Arrange the letters, placing narrow background strips in between to act as spacers as shown in the assembly diagram. Sew the letters and spacers together to make the word; press and trim.

7. Sew a medium background strip to the top edge of the word; press toward the background strip and trim. Sew medium background strips to the bottom, left, and right edges, pressing and trimming after adding each strip.

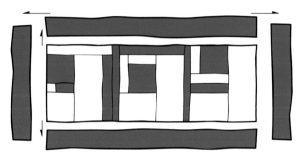

Assembly diagram

8. Sew a 4½"-wide border strip to the left edge of the quilt; press toward the border and trim. Sew 4½"-wide border strips to the right, top, and bottom edges, pressing and trimming after adding each strip.

Finishing

1. Layer the backing, batting, and quilt top; baste.

2. Hand or machine quilt as desired.

3. Join the 1½"-wide strips and use them to finish the edges of the quilt.

"BIRDIE JOY," 20" x 23½", 2001, designed, made, and hand quilted in freehand fans by the author. The word _Joy_ was made the same way as for "Christmas Joy" (page 53).

BOO

"BOO WITH SKELETONS," 21" x 20", 2009, designed, made,
and hand quilted with pearl cotton by the author.

Materials

Yardages given are based on a quilt that finishes
the approximate size of the sample and—with the
exception of fat quarters—are based on fabric that
measures approximately 40" wide.

⅓ yard of fabric for border

Fat quarter *each* of 2 contrasting fabrics for letters
    and background (including equalizer and
    spacers)*

⅞ yard of fabric for backing

Fat quarter of fabric for binding

27" x 26" piece of batting

*If you prefer, you can select an additional fat
quarter of a novelty Halloween print for the top area
of the background.

Cutting

Cutting the strips in the dimensions below will
give you a word that finishes approximately 5" tall
as shown in the sample quilt. Of course, you can
change the strip widths or lengths that you use for
each letter if you like. Changing strip measurements
will change the size of the word, so you'll need to
adjust the yardage for background, borders, and
backing and the size of the batting accordingly. Cut
additional letter and background strips if you need
them.

From the background fabric, cut:
    1 strip, 1½" wide
    1 piece, 17" x 8½"**

From the letter fabric, cut:
    1 narrow strip, 1¼" wide
    1 medium strip, 2" wide
    1 wide strip, 2½" wide

From the border fabric, cut:
    1 strip, 2½" x 40"
    1 strip, 3¾ x 40"

From the backing fabric, cut:
    1 piece, 26" x 27"

From the binding fabric, cut:
    5 strips", 1½" x 20"+

**If you choose an additional fat quarter of a novelty Halloween print for the background, use it for this piece.

+For single-fold binding that finishes approximately ⅜" wide.

Making the Quilt Top

Refer to "UnRuly Letter Basics" (page 13) and "Working with Words" (page 38) as needed. The area of background fabric above the word is a great place to show your prowess at quilting or to use a wonderful novelty print. I just cut a piece in a size that looked good to me. I went with uneven borders because I wanted the quilt to have an impact from a distance where you might not see the quilting. There was no mathematical calculation behind the border widths—I just auditioned different sizes by folding my border fabric and then picked what I liked. You can use my measurements or choose your own.

1. Beginning with a square cut from the background strip, make the first capital O (page 21). Use narrow letter strips for the top and right edges, and wide letter strips for the bottom and left edges.

2. Make the second O, this time beginning with a 3"-long rectangle cut from the background strip. Use narrow letter strips for the top and bottom, and medium letter strips for the sides.

3. The *B* in this quilt is a little bit different from the one on page 24. Start the top unit with a square cut from the background strip (1). Refer to the diagram below and use narrow letter strips for 2 and 3, pressing and trimming as you add each piece. Finish by sewing a background strip to the right edge (4); press and trim.

4. Start with a 2½"-long rectangle cut from the background strip (A) for the bottom unit. Refer to the diagram below and use narrow letter strips for B and C, and a medium letter strip for D, pressing and trimming as you add each piece.

5. Sew the unit from step 3 to the top edge of the unit from step 4; press. Sew a wide letter strip to the left edge; press and trim to finish the letter.

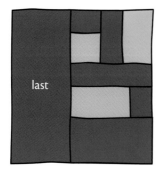

6. Refer to "Making Letters 'Dance'" (page 39) and add background equalizer strips so that all letter units are the same height. Press, and trim as needed.

7. Arrange the letters, placing background strips in between for spacers as shown in the assembly diagram. Sew the letters and spacers together to make the word; press and trim.

8. Sew a strip of background fabric to the left edge of the unit from step 7; press toward the background strip and trim. Sew background strips to the right and bottom edges, pressing and trimming after adding each strip. Finish by sewing the 17" x 8½" piece of background fabric to the top; press toward the background piece. **Note:** If you're using a novelty print for the 17" x 8½" piece, you may want to add a strip of background fabric to the top of *BOO* before attaching the novelty print.

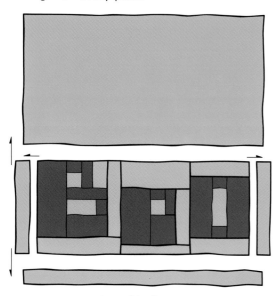

Assembly diagram

9. Sew a 2½"-wide border strip to the bottom edge of the quilt; press toward the border and trim. Sew a 3¾"-wide border strip to the left edge, a 2½"-wide border strip to the right edge, and a 3¾"-wide border strip to the top edge, pressing and trimming after adding each strip.

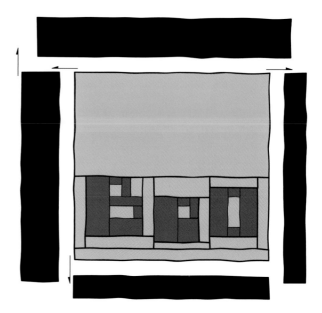

Finishing

1. Layer the backing, batting, and quilt top; baste.

2. Hand or machine quilt as desired.

3. Join the 1½"-wide strips and use them to finish the edges of the quilt.

VOTE

"VOTE," 16½" x 15½", 2009, designed, made, and hand quilted in wavy lines by the author.

Materials

Yardages given are based on a quilt that finishes the approximate size of the sample. A row of stripes under the stars would make the section look even more like a flag; also see "America with Flag" (page 42).

Fat quarter *each of 2 contrasting fabrics for letters and background*

Fat quarter of star fabric for upper-left quilt top

Fat quarter of striped fabric for upper-right quilt top

⅔ yard of fabric for backing

Fat quarter of fabric for binding

22" x 21" piece of batting

Cutting

Cutting strips in the dimensions listed will yield a word that finishes approximately 5" tall (although not all the letters are that height) x 12" wide as shown in the sample quilt. The letters in this quilt are skinnier and taller than those in the previous projects. Change the strip widths or lengths if you like. Changing strip measurements will change the size of the word, so adjust the yardage for the backing and the size of the batting accordingly. Cut additional letter and background strips if needed.

From the background fabric, cut:
   1 narrow strip, 1" wide
   1 medium strip, 1½" wide
   2 wide strips, 2" wide
   2 strips, 2½" x 20"

From the letter fabric, cut:
   1 narrow strip, 1" wide
   1 medium strip, 1½" wide

From the star fabric, cut:
 1 piece, 8" x 10"

From the striped fabric, cut:
 1 piece, 8" x 7"

From the backing fabric, cut:
 1 piece, 22" x 21"

From the binding fabric, cut:
 4 strips, 1½" x 20"*

For single-fold binding that finishes approximately ⅜" wide.

Making the Quilt Top

Refer to "UnRuly Letter Basics" (page 13) and "Working with Words" (page 38) as needed.

1. Beginning with a 3½"-long rectangle cut from the medium background strip, make a capital O (page 21). Use narrow letter strips for the top and left edges, and medium letter strips for the bottom and right edges.

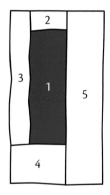

2. Beginning with a 5½"-long rectangle cut from the medium letter strip (1), make a lowercase *t* (page 33). Refer to "Inserting Strips" (page 16) to insert a narrow letter strip at an angle (3).

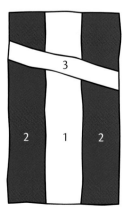

3. The *E* in this quilt is a little bit different from the one I showed you in "Capital E" (page 23). Cut a 1½"-long rectangle (1) from the narrow letter strip and a square from the narrow background strip (2). Sew the square to the end of the rectangle; press. Sew this unit between a narrow background strip and the end of a wide background strip as shown; press and trim the unit to approximately 3½".

4. Sew a narrow letter strip to the top and a medium letter strip to the bottom of the unit from step 3; press and trim. Sew a medium letter strip to the left edge; press and trim.

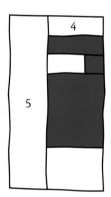

5. To make the V (page 28), cut a 4"-long rectangle from the wide background strip to make a long triangle. Use a medium letter strip to add the left leg of the V (2), and a narrow letter strip to add the right leg (3).

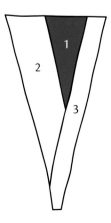

6. Refer to "Duplicating an Angle" (page 18), and use wide background strips to duplicate the angles on the left and right edges of the *V*. Trim the extra background fabric on the sides so that ½" extends beyond the top of the *V* on both sides.

7. Add background equalizer strips (for example, to the top of *O* and *E*) so that all letter units are the same height. Press, and trim as needed.

8. Arrange the letters, placing narrow background strips between *O* and *t* and between *t* and *E* for spacers as shown in the assembly diagram. Sew the letters and spacers together to make the word; press and trim.

9. Sew a 2½"-wide background strip to the left edge of the word; press toward the background strip. Sew a 2½"-wide background strip to the right edge, a medium background strip to the top edge, and a wide background strip to the bottom edge, pressing and trimming after adding each strip.

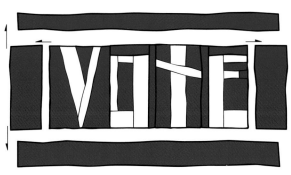

Assembly diagram

10. Sew the star piece and the striped piece together along their 8" edges as shown below; press. Center and sew the unit to the top edge of the unit from step 9; press toward the word. Trim any excess to even the quilt edges.

Finishing

1. Layer the backing, batting, and quilt top; baste.

2. Hand or machine quilt as desired.

3. Join the 1½"-wide strips and use them to finish the edges of the quilt.

LETTER AND NUMBER CHARTS

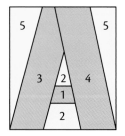
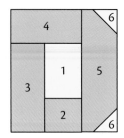
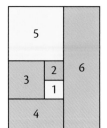
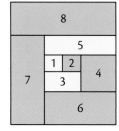
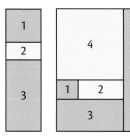
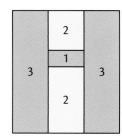
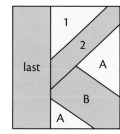
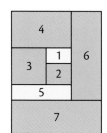
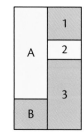
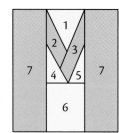
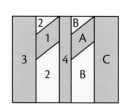
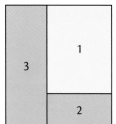

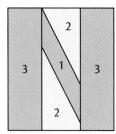
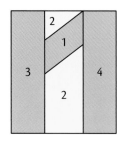

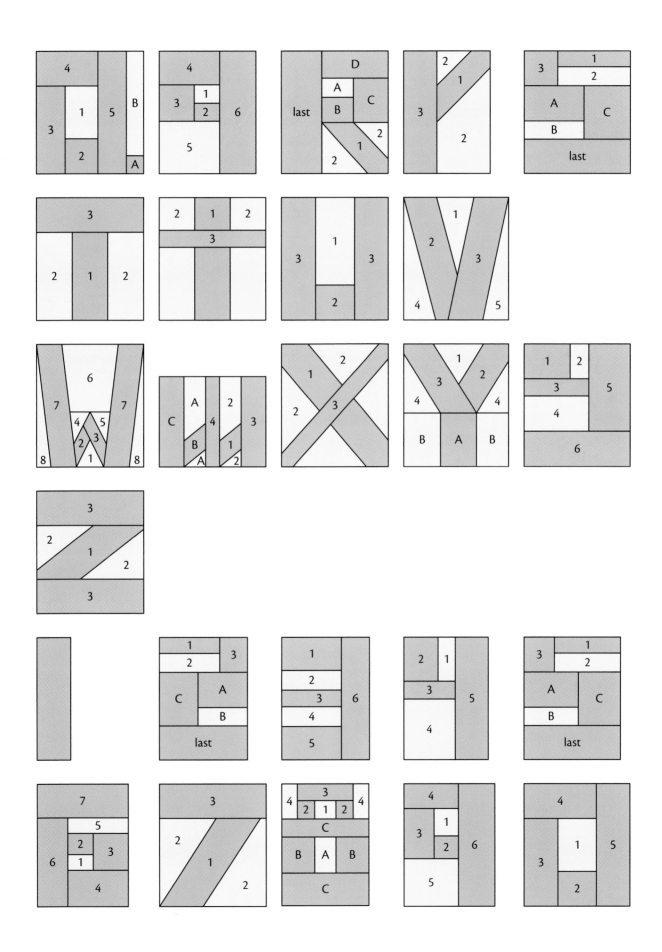

RESOURCES

Better Homes and Gardens. *America's Heritage Quilts*. Des Moines, IA: Meredith Corporation, 1991.

Marston, Gwen. *Liberated Quiltmaking*. Paducah, KY: American Quilter's Society, 1996.

———. *Liberated Quiltmaking II*. Paducah, KY: American Quilter's Society, 2010.

The Alzheimer's Art Quilt Initiative (AAQI): www.alzquilts.org.

Heartstrings Quilt Project: www.heartstringsquiltproject.com.

ACKNOWLEDGMENTS

Huge amounts of thanks go to:

Gwen Marston, without whom I'd never have ventured so far. Thank you for Liberated Quiltmaking as well as your mentorship and friendship.

Bonnie K. Hunter, for putting my letter-making tutorials on her website Quiltville. Otherwise those tutorials would have disappeared into my blog archives.

Darra Williamson, for her encouragement, patience, and editorial prowess. I'd have had a nervous breakdown without her.

Diane Burdin, who did an amazing job helping me get this manuscript in shape. She read and commented over and over and over again with nary a complaint.

Siobhan Furgurson and Brenda Suderman, for reading my first draft.

The quilters who've shared their work in this book, as well as those whose quilts didn't make it. Believe me, I wish I could have included them all.

And last but not least, to all the wonderful people who've read and commented on my blog, as well as the quilters who've sent me blocks and/or photos of their wonderful free-pieced-letters quilts.

ABOUT THE AUTHOR

TONYA RICUCCI is a fortysomething stay-at-home mom to four cats, adopted by Tonya and her husband from the streets of Cairo, Egypt. They're well-traveled cats, as they've also lived with the couple in two U.S. states and in Paris, France. All are currently living in Florida.

Tonya has been quilting for more than 20 years, focusing on Liberated and UnRuly quiltmaking and letters for the last 10.

THERE'S MORE ONLINE!

- For tutorials on free-piecing and hand quilting, photos of quilts made by Tonya and her students, and more, visit UnrulyQuilter.com.

- Find out what's new with Tonya at her blog, www.lazygalquilting.blogspot.com.

- Discover more great quilt books at www.martingale-pub.com.